The ABC's of Apostleship

An Introductory Overview
"Apostleship From God to You"

STUDENT WORKBOOK 1
UNITS 1-6

PAULA A. PRICE, PHD

The ABC's of Apostleship

An Introductory Overview
"Apostleship From God to You"

STUDENT WORKBOOK 1
UNITS 1-6

Unless otherwise indicated, all scriptural quotations are from the King James Version of the Bible. Scripture verses marked NKJV are taken from the Holy Bible, New King James Version, © 1973, 1978, 1984 by the International Bible Society. Used by permission of Zondervan Publishing House.

ABC's of Apostleship: Apostleship from God to You
Student Workbook1 – Units 1-6
Flaming Vision Publications
Tulsa, Oklahoma 74136
ISBN 1-886288-08-9

Printed in the United States of America

This workbook belongs to:

_____

Class or Study Name:

_____

Organization or Ministry:

_____

Class/Semester Date:

_____

Teacher

_____

Your Workbook Outline

About Your Student Workbook

As Book 1 one of a two book series, this workbook lays the foundation for Book 2 by giving you the rudiments of New Testament apostleship. It contains 6 of the 18 units in this volume of the *ABC's of Apostleship* Series. Books 2 and 3 build on Book 1 knowledge by opening up the subject further and taking you deeper into its explanations. As you study apostleship using this book, you will obtain the introductory insights you need to awaken you to what the Lord Jesus brought into His kingdom and set over His New Testament church. The *ABC's of Apostleship* student workbook is written to go with its textbook of the same title. As with the textbook, the workbook too is written with you in mind. Arranged for you to work out the textbook's wisdom through a variety of activities and exercises related to apostleship, the workbook guides your step by step study of the apostle's ministry. Many of the workbook's unit studies, lectures, and discussions come from the textbook's Unit End Summaries.

The greatest value this workbook has to offer the church's pastors and ministries is that it is ideally suited to group study. Everyone in the church today can benefit from its systematic lessons on apostleship. As a learning and teaching tool this textbook companion is useful for Adult Bible Study classes, apostolic and prophetic learning groups and classes, church leadership and their congregations, as well as individuals. Newly appointed or installed apostles and apostolic churches will find it indispensable as a guide to transitioning their ministries to apostleship. The volumes in the series contains as little as three and as many as five workbooks. Sequentially numbered, the workbooks progressively guide a church or student's apostleship studies. Divided into six units each, every individual workbook is uniformly organized for continuity. The units link primary subject matter to the same title in the textbook, so that they go hand in hand. You can take notes from your lectures, work on assigned exercises and work out the material you learn right in your workbook. Everything you finish in your studies is always there for you to review and refresh yourself on what you learned about apostleship. To understand how your workbook is designed, you should read the following information carefully to get the best out of your apostleship study.

When you start a new unit in the textbook your workbook will guide you through it step by step. Every unit in your workbook contains the following:

STANDARD UNIT ELEMENTS

Every unit in your workbook contains the following elements for uniformity and unity.

1. **UNIT GOAL** – *To tell you the unit's aim and purpose.*

2. **UNIT OBJECTIVES** – *To list for you what the unit will accomplish.*

3. **KEY UNIT POINTS** – *To outline what you will come across when studying the unit.*

4. **SCRIPTURE FOCUS** – *To supply you with the scriptures[1] that support unit teachings.*

5. **UNIT KEYWORDS** – *To give you the most important words to remember from the unit.*

6. **IMPORTANT UNIT DISCUSSION POINTS** – *To point out for you the topics your lectures will cover in the unit.*

7. **ACTIVITY LEARNING VALUE*** – *To explain for you the skill value of assigned exercises.*

8. **UNIT PRACTICE EXERCISE*** – *To describe for you the related situations the unit has for you to practice what you learn.*

9. **WHAT YOU SHOULD KNOW** – *To identify for you what the unit expects you to obtain and remember most from its study.*

10. **UNIT END SUMMARY** – *To recall for you the main points of the entire unit.*

11. **NOTE TO SELF*** – *A learning task that reinforces a significant study idea for you.*

12. **SELF CHECKER*** – *A series of questions that challenge what you presently believe or know about the particular aspect of apostleship addressed.*

13. **SCENARIOS*** – *Real-like issues that you work on using your newfound wisdom.*

---

[1] All scripture is taken from the KJV Bible.

14. **SIMULATIONS*** – *Specially chosen situations that you act out to refine your apostleship knowledge before giving others the unit's insights.*

15. **KNOWLEDGE REFLECTIONS*** – *Thoughts and considerations meant to inspire you to reflect on the entire unit's premises and teachings.*

16. **GAMES*** – *Fun ways for you to test skill, abilities, and application of the unit's facts, teachings, and practicalities.*

17. **WORKSHEETS*** – *Study and practice tools to aid homework and coursework.*[2]

You should stake the time to read and learn all of the 17 Standard Unit Elements described above. Not all of them show up in every unit. Those that do not are marked with an (*). Expect to see and use the elements throughout your *ABC's of Apostleship* learning experience. In addition to the above, there are the unit's *Tidbits, Doctrends* and *Myth-Conceptions*. These are scattered throughout the workbook, and not all units have them. These interesting additions round out your learning of a unit's theme.

WORKBOOK UNIT ARRANGEMENTS

All units' contents are arranged to help you comprehend what you read and study about apostleship. You do not want to skip a single unit in your textbook or your workbook because every part helps you learn all that you should about the Lord's apostleship. You also do not want to pass over any of the learning assignments or do them without the learning tools the workbook provides. All of the content and supplements of your workbook collectively aid your in-depth study of apostles, apostolic ministry, apostleship and your role in them all. So, pay close attention to unit goals and objectives. Read all instructions thoroughly and follow them carefully. Take time to fix the Important Discussion Points clearly in your mind. Do not rush through them, or any of the material just to finish. The Keyword Studies and scripture recommendations set the tone of the unit. They prepare your mind for what is taught. As you can see, each unit element or feature serves a definite purpose and adds value to your study. All of them were specially chosen to progressively strengthen your appreciation and understanding of apostleship.

---

[2] Not all units contain this element.

SPECIAL UNIT SUPPLEMENTS

The Special Unit Supplements expand your learning potential and permit you to apply your understanding in realistic ways. For example, take "The Active Learning Values." They give you the reason for an exercise or activity. The Tidbits provide little clues into the unit's main thought. "The Doctrends" identify a carnal worldview or piece of pop theology the unit explores. And, then there are the "Myth-Conceptions." These expose flaws in your beliefs or conception of apostleship as compared to the unit's teachings. "The Note to Self" is a popup reminder that tells you to do some follow up activity that reinforces or verifies what you learn. "The Self Checkers" list personal statements related to the teachings that question your perspectives on a topic of apostleship studied. "The Knowledge Reflections" ask you to contemplate your newfound knowledge as you make it your own revelation. The scenarios depict situations and cases where your knowledge can be applied. The simulations let you practice what you learn in apostolic situations or settings. To further enrich your educational process, there are the word games. They test your skill, information recall, and knowledge retention.

The ABC's of Apostleship course so informs you on apostleship that you will be able to arrive at your own conclusions about it. When you finish each workbook in the series, you will be armed to answer apostleship questions yourself. You will also be able to rightly judge true from false apostleship and settle once and for all in your own heart and mind if it is of God or not. In addition, you will know if you should get involved with it as His child. All in all an exciting learning experience awaits you as you personally unlock the mysteries of apostleship for yourself.

SUGGESTED USE OF THIS WORKBOOK

To help you get the most from your *ABC's of Apostleship* learning experience, here are some suggestions for using your workbook. Your workbook is full of a variety of materials that are designed to simplify your study of this subject. Its contents are structured to be handled systematically to progress you through the successive stages of apostleship learning. It is suggested that you go through this material unit by unit so that introductory knowledge is properly built upon. Plan to engage in your studies at the same time each day or week. If you are a school, you will probably want to use this material as part of an established curriculum. If so, most likely you will meet once or twice a week. If that is the case, then it will take you about 8-12 weeks to go through the workbook. If you are a church or ministry, you are probably meeting once per week, which means you should schedule your sessions to last approximately twice as long. As an individual, your self paced study of this book is at your discretion. Still, you should go through it systematically and expect to allow yourself at least 2 hours a day a couple of times per week to get through it. Self paced learners will need about 8 to 12 weeks to complete the workbook and all of its assignments.

The best way to approach this workbook is by going through it side by side with the textbook. Begin by reading The Standard Unit Elements, reviewing the Workbook Unit Arrangements and the Special Unit Supplements. These give you a sense of the nature and order of the workbook. The most important of the three are the Standard Unit Elements that open up every unit. Do not just skim over the goals and objectives, Key Discussion Points, Scripture Focus, Keywords or What You Should Know & Be Able to Do from the unit. They set the tone and prepare your mind for what is being taught. Typically, teachers use these in tests, reviews, or other reinforcement exercises to ensure that you soundly understand and can apply what you learn. When you come to one of the many exercises in the workbook, such as the Keyword Studies, Bonus Questions or Word Activities, be sure to stay on topic and use the unit's teachings in your responses. If you are a class, The Important Unit Discussions will generally guide your instructor's teaching of the text. They underscore what you should note from your lectures. Lastly, there are the Unit Review Questions. These test your comprehension and cement your studies in your mind. You are strongly urged to follow the recommended format in your approach to this material. Doing so will help you glean the most from your journey into the ABC's of Apostleship.

God bless you and stay open to learn and glean the answers to your questions yourself.

BOOK ONE

UNIT 1

Welcome to the ABC's of Apostleship

UNIT CONTENTS

Introduction
The Missing Link
You and This Series
Defining Apostleship
The Purpose of this Book

UNIT GOAL

The goal of this unit is to launch you into your apostleship journey so that it makes sense to you the everyday Christian.

UNIT OBJECTIVES

This unit has 6 objectives, which are:

> **Unit Tidbit:**
> "Understanding why apostleship is a divine commission instead of just a string of international missions further differentiates it from the other offices."

1. To introduce you to apostleship by exploring biblical and early church apostleship.
2. To lay the foundation for the unit's study with definitions, keywords and scripture studies.
3. To teach you what makes apostleship important to God.
4. To show you how and why apostleship has suffered so in the Lord's house.
5. To teach you God's brand of apostleship.
6. To condition you, the everyday Christian to discuss, understand and appreciate apostleship in the church.

SIGNIFICANT IDEAS TO STRESS:

The key discussion points of this unit are:

1. The people apostles are being raised up to affect and empower have little to no idea of who they are, what they do, and why apostles are important to their lives.
2. Many members of the body of Christ have never come across the term "apostle" outside of scripture, if at all.
3. Studying your Bible along with this study guide biblically connects you with apostleship to make it and God make sense to you in your world.
4. It is helpful to you to learn why apostleship is important to God.
5. You should know what makes apostles first in the Lord's ministry orders on earth and in heaven.
6. The words apostleship and apostolic are not the same thing.

SCRIPTURE FOCUS

Throughout your study of this unit, you will focus on the following scriptures:

- 1 Corinthians 12:28
- Hebrews 12:22-24
- Acts 26:18
- 1 Peter 2:9
- John 14:15-21; Romans 5:10,11
- 2 Corinthians 5:17-20; Galatians 2:20
- Genesis 1:26; Colossians 21:2-4
- Rev 21:2-4

UNIT KEYWORDS

The words you want to learn the most about in this unit are:

- Apostleship
- Apostolic
- "Doctrends"
- Myth-Conception
- Reconciliation
- Compatible
- Prototypical
- Mantle
- Ministry
- Ministerial
- Ambassadorial
- Agents

   ◆   Ambassadorship

WHAT YOU SHOULD KNOW OR BE ABLE TO DO FROM THIS UNIT

To actualize your knowledge from this unit, you should embody the following things:

1. How the Unit Goal is recognized in action.
2. What each objective requires in order to manifest its wisdom.
3. How to turn the *Significant Ideas to Stress* into action.
4. How to apply the Unit Scriptures
5. The ways the Keywords help your understanding of apostleship.
6. The definition of the word apostle.
7. How apostleship differs from apostolic.

UNIT 1: SIGNIFICANT IDEAS TO STRESS

As you read your text and go through this unit, you want to pay particular attention to:

1. A glaring void exists in the Lord's twenty or so year effort to shift His church's primary leadership to apostles.

2. You, the everyday Christian, have to know apostleship from God's mind to your world, not the other way around.

3. The people that apostles are being raised up to affect and empower have little to no idea of who they are, what they do, and why apostles are important to their lives.

4. Because apostleship is essential to God, it is first in God's ministry orders on earth and in heaven according 1 Corinthians 12:28.

5. Many members of the body of Christ have never come across the term "apostle" outside of scripture.

17

6. Studying your Bible along with this study guide biblically connects you with apostleship to make it and God's use of apostles make sense to you and your world.

7. The word Apostleship surpasses the word apostolic in dignity and effect.

8. Apostleship is a divine commission instead of just a string of international missions.

9. Apostleship's most apparent power is its population, preservation, and perpetuation of God's kingdom on earth.

10. To apostles the ecclesia is more than the church in the same way that a kingdom is more than its temple.

UNIT 1: KEYWORD STUDY

Activity Learning Value:

The learning value of this exercise is your increased ability to discuss apostleship intelligently using words that paint an accurate and credible picture of it from the Lord's point of view and not from traditional commentaries.

Student: *Use this study aid to help you gain a broader understanding of the keywords found in this unit. Apply each keyword in different ways to show how you recognize their relevance.*

Definition Study Chart		
Keyword or Term	**Definition: Source A**	**Definition: Source B**

List the scripture references related to your keyword(s):

1. _____

2. _____

3. _____

4. _____

Related Words Chart

<u>**Explanation:**</u> The terms and synonyms that you enter below show your research of this unit's assigned words.

Keyword or Term	Synonym(s)

Word Origins Chart

Explanation: The words you enter below show your grasp of the words you searched out and how they are to be used in apostleship discussions.

Origin of Term	Original Use	Modern Use	Scriptural Use

How is this word(s) used in this unit's study?

Term Purpose	Term Relevance	Skill Knowledge & Value

What is the scripture application?

What is their application to this unit study?

Explanation of Summary Statement Tasks: This task is to enable you to take what you learn from research and phrase it for communicating apostleship to family and friends.

Summary Statement: *(Give a one-statement summary of what you have learned about your keywords and phrases)*

Three Main Revelations You Received:

What would you say is the value of this study to you, the Lord and His church?

UNIT 1: PRACTICE EXERCISE # 1

FILLING IN THE RIGHT WORD

Activity Learning Value:

The learning value of this exercise is your recognition of and connection with the most effective apostolic words that define it understandably for others.

Using your book and lecture notes, locate the missing word or phrase in each statement.

1. Many members of the body of Christ have never come across the term "____"outside of scripture.

    a. ecclesia

2. Why apostleship is about gods and _____ and how their distinct message and doctrine verifies them is what you will learn from this teaching.

    b. commission

3. Understanding why apostleship is a divine _____ instead of just a string of international missions further differentiates it from the other offices.

    c. ABC's

4. True apostleship thrives on kingship and _____ to increase your appreciation of its kingdom doctrines.

    d. apostle

5. How apostleship is God's tool of _____

    e. compatible

6. To apostles the _____ is more than the church.

    f. nations

7. These ____ explain how and why we are the Almighty's promised nation of kings and priests to Christ's God.

    g. reconciliation

8. How apostleship makes you _____with God

    h. ambassadorship

    i. holiness

UNIT 1: PRACTICE EXERCISE #2

Getting You Ready to Think Differently About Apostles and Apostleship

Apostleship as God's impending era is fast coming upon Christianity, its churches and ministers, and the world. In a very short time you will be faced with, and forced to answer, how it works, how to tell the true from the false, and what may be expected of an apostle's ministry in your life.

Value of Activity

The value of this activity is your awakened understanding and eventual insight in the apostleship as it is to manifest, operate, and produce in the life of a Christian, the world of the church, the mantles of its officers, along with its world impact for Jesus Christ.

Think Tank

Spend time as a study group, a class, or a circle of trusted peers brainstorming and working through what actualizes a determined Christian's pursuit apostleship's three 'G' mandate, how it would be recognized in action, considered successful and what its end product would look like, do, and achieve on the Lord's behalf.

UNIT 1: REVIEW QUESTIONS

To wrap up your study of this unit, answer the following questions.

1. What does apostleship mean?

2. How does the word apostleship differ from the word apostolic in thought and action?

3. What does an apostle do for the Lord and the church?

4. How does apostleship make you compatible with God?

5. How is apostleship God's tool of reconciliation?

6. Why must apostleship reveal Jesus Christ?

7. Who is apostleship's central focus?

8. Why is apostleship not a fad?

9. What does apostleship exist to do?

10. Why is apostleship a divine commission?

11. How does 1 Corinthians 12:28 substantiate apostleship?

12. How would you walk out the goal of apostleship as taught in this unit?

13. How would you demonstrate at least 3 of the unit's objectives in action for those who need to see apostleship at work to understand it?

BONUS

As a personal test of your new knowledge of apostleship, do the following assignment. If you are a class, and if your responses are good, you should receive extra credit for it.

Use a minimum of 4 of the unit's keywords in a statement that says what it is about in your own words. That is according to your present understanding.

UNIT 1: STUDENT LECTURE NOTES

Students: *Use this page for additional lecture notes.*

UNIT 2

The Almighty's Apostleship

UNIT CONTENTS
The A, B, & C of Apostleship
Ambassadorship & Apostleship

UNIT GOAL

The goal of this unit is to bring you into the world of the Godhead's apostleship so that you are comfortable with God's approved apostles and comprehend their purpose and value to Jesus and His church.

UNIT OBJECTIVES

This unit has 4 objectives, which are:

1. To actualize the unit's goal for you
2. To begin the process of helping you grasp the ABC's of Apostleship.
3. To enable you to relate ambassadorship to God's Apostleship.
4. To make the 'A' connection in the ABC's of Apostleship for you.

SIGNIFICANT UNIT IDEAS TO STRESS

> **UNIT TIDBIT:**
>
> "[Ambassadorship] is the world's counterpart to the church's apostle."

The key discussion points of this unit are:

1. Apostles, what they are: A working definition.
2. Crystallizing apostleship for you from God's point of view.
3. Making apostleship make sense to you from God's mind.
4. What precisely makes ambassadors the highest ranking diplomatic officials of their state.

SCRIPTURE FOCUS

Throughout your study of this unit, you will focus on the following scriptures:

- 2 Corinthians 5:17
- Ephesians 3:1; 6:20
- Philippians 1:1, 7, 13, 16
- Philemon 1:1, 9, 10, 13
- Jude 1
- Colossians 4:3, 18
- 2 Timothy 2:19
- Hebrews 10:34; 11:36

UNIT KEYWORDS

The words you want to learn the most about in this unit are:

- Ambassadors
- Apostleship
- Bondservant
- Commission
- Commissioned
- Messengers
- Throne
- Representative
- Diplomatic agent
- Rank
- Sovereign
- Sent one
- Missionaries
- Accredit

REMEMBER YOUR APOSTLESHIP ABC'S:

A=Apostleship

B=Bondservant

C=Commissioned

WHAT YOU SHOULD KNOW OR BE ABLE TO DO FROM THIS UNIT

To actualize your knowledge form this unit, you should embody the following things:

1. The word *apostleship* as it pertains to the *officiaries* of an "apostle's *dignities*. See your textbook for the meaning of this word.
2. What makes apostles the Lord's special class of high ranking New Testament ministers.
3. What makes apostles the Godhead's highest ambassadorial messengers.
4. How the Lord sends His apostles from eternity's throne.
5. What is involved in apostles represent the Godhead on earth.
6. The value of your rudimentary apostleship knowledge to the Lord's apostleship reinstatement efforts.
7. How the A, B, & C in the unit makes the book's point.
8. What diplomacy and ambassadorship have to do with the Lord Jesus' apostleship.
9. The role, duties, and functions of apostleship.
10. How apostleship serves as the Almighty's counterpart to the world's senior diplomatic agent.
11. How apostleship is to build relations with world powers on the Most High God's behalf.
12. Why God needs ambassadors and diplomats in His church, and among His ministerial staff.
13. What it means to the church to know that apostles like ambassadors are the highest ranking diplomatic officials of their state
14. How apostles meet the ambassadorship criterion of being sent by the head of their state to the heads of world nations.

UNIT 2: SIGNIFICANT IDEAS TO STRESS

As you read your text and go through this unit, you want to pay particular attention to:

1. What makes apostles the Lord's special class of high ranking New Testament ministers.

_____

_____

_____

2. What qualifies apostles to be the Godhead's highest ambassadorial messengers.

_____

_____

_____

3. Why the alphabet is used in the study's title.

_____

_____

_____

4. How apostles biblically represent the Godhead on earth.

_____

_____

_____

5. The tangible value you would place on your rudimentary knowledge of apostleship to the Lord's apostleship reinstatement efforts from this unit's treatment of it.

_____

_____

_____

6. How apostles are sent from eternity's throne to represent it in the earth."

_____

_____

_____

7. Three ways this book makes apostleship sensitizes your to apostleship based on the Lord's perspective of it.

_____

_____

_____

8. Unlatching the unit's A, B, and C foundations.

_____

_____

_____

9. The fourth letter of the study's ABC's and how it ties it all together.

_____

_____

_____

10. What ambassadors as the highest ranking diplomatic officials of their state achieve for their sending states, which is...?

_____

_____

_____

_____

REMEMBER YOUR APOSTLESHIP ABC'S:

A=Apostleship

B=Bondservant

C=Commissioned

KEYWORD STUDY: AMBASSADORSHIP

Student: *Use this study aid to help you gain a broader understanding of the keywords found in this unit. Apply each keyword in different ways to show how you recognize their relevance.*

Definition Study Chart		
Keyword or Term	**Definition: Source A**	**Definition: Source B**

List the scripture references related to your keyword(s):

1. _____
2. _____
3. _____
4. _____

Related Words Chart

Keyword or Term	Synonym(s)

Word Origins Chart

Origin of Term	Original Use	Modern Use	Scriptural Use

How is this word(s) used in this unit's study?

Term Purpose	Term Relevance	Skill Knowledge & Value

What is the scripture application?

What is their application to this unit study?

Summary Statement: *(Give a one-statement summary of what you have learned about your keywords and phrases)*

Three Main Revelations You Received:

What would you say is the value of this study to you, the Lord and His church?

ACTION ITEM[3]

Describe or depict how you would make what you just learned understandable to someone who knows nothing about apostleship. Conclude with the signs or comments you would like to see or hear to confirm that you selected and used the most understandable terms to communicate this unit's material successfully.

If you are a study group or class, share your ideas with the group and review your group's responses and outcomes below:

_____

[3] **Activity Learning Value:** The fulfillment of the priority goals and objectives of this training that propose to enable you to discuss apostleship intelligently within your circle of friends, family and acquaintances.

UNIT 2: PRACTICE EXERCISE

This exercise has multiple parts that may be assigned and addressed all at once or separately.

Part One: Unit two outlines the functions and duties of the ambassador as they relate the similarities of their duties and functions of God's apostles.

Part Two: Compare and contrast your understanding of the apostle as an ambassador to how you previously understood ambassadors to function.

Part Three: Include in your answer, a discussion of these important points:

A. How you see apostles working and serving as present-day ambassadors.

B. How you would explain to a friend the wide range of duties apostles God assigned apostleship as His highest New Testament ministry office.

C. The particular things you would now say makes apostles different and confirms they are just like ambassadors.

Special Practice Exercise

FILLING IN THE RIGHT WORD

Who Am I?

Activity Learning Value:

The learning value of this exercise is your recognition of and connection with the most effective apostolic words that distinguish apostleship from ambassadorship for others.

Using your book and lecture notes, enter the missing word or phrase in column 2 for each of the statements below.

What I Do	**Who Am I**
1. I am sent from the head of my state to the heads of foreign countries. _____	**A.** Bondservant
2. I speak to other nations for my national leader. _____	**B.** Commission
3. I represent the Godhead's sovereignty in the earth. _____	**C.** Sent One
4. I refer to the most basic teachings of a subject. _____	**D.** Missionary
5. When I go out in my sender's name I am given a? _____	**E.** Messenger
6. I am a high ranking slave to my sender. _____	**F.** Diplomat
7. I travel to foreign lands, but I am not an ambassador or apostle. _____	**G.** Ambassador
8. When my leader tells me to take a communications to someone, I function as a _____	**H.** Apostle
9. My primary purpose is to convey others thoughts and ideas. _____	**I.** ABC's
	J. Diplomatic Agent

UNIT 2: REVIEW QUESTIONS

To wrap up your study of this unit, answer the following questions.

1. Apostleship involves three main things. What are they and how might one detect them in action?

_____

_____

_____

2. When you hear or see the word apostleship, what you are dealing with pertains to _____?

3. In your understanding, what makes apostles the Lord's special class of high ranking New Testament ministers?

_____

_____

_____

4. What do apostles do that unmistakably manifests them as the Godhead's highest ambassadorial messengers?

_____

_____

_____

5. How does the Lord send His apostles from His eternal throne?

_____

_____

_____

6. What would you say is involved in apostles' representing the Godhead on earth?

_____

_____

7. Give your perception of the worth of wide spread rudimentary knowledge of apostleship to the Lord's apostleship reinstatement efforts.

8. What would you say to others who ask you how apostleship serves as the Almighty's counterpart to the world's senior diplomatic agent.

9. What makes the Godhead need a diplomatic corps or senior diplomatic agents?

10. With Christ's church in mind, how are apostles to build relations with world powers on the Most High God's behalf?

11. In respect to apostleship, what does it mean for the Lord's church to grasp the reality that apostleship resembles ambassadorship.

12. What accredits ambassadors as the highest ranking diplomatic officials of their state?

_____

_____

_____

13. What accredits apostles as the highest ranking diplomatic officials of God's kingdom?

_____

_____

_____

14. How do apostles meet the ambassadorial criteria of their posts that require them to be sent by the head of their state to the heads of world nations?

_____

_____

_____

15. This unit discusses apostleship as encompassing what two commonly known agents?

_____

16. The first letter in our ABC's, 'A' stands for_____ in the series title?

17. The second letter in our ABC's B stands for_____ in the series title?

18. The third letter in our ABC's 'C' stands for _____ in the series title?

19. What are ambassadors sent to do?

_____

20. What separates apostles from ambassadors?

_____

BONUS⁴

This is a 2 part Assignment that may be given together or separately.

As a personal test of your new knowledge of apostleship, do the following assignment. If you are a class, you should receive extra credit for it, if your responses are good.

Part One: What scriptures in the Bible support your answers to A, B, and C above?

\
\
\

Part Two: List three things that you need to see or hear to tell you that you were successful in communicating or demonstrating your newfound apostleship knowledge. (Depending upon what you intend for others to get from your response, alternate as necessary using such words as "wisdom", insight, skill, awareness, recognition or perception.)

1.

2.

3.

---

⁴ **Activity Learning Value**: To equip you to discuss apostleship from more than a Christian or church perspective in a variety of settings.

UNIT 2: STUDENT LECTURE NOTES

Students: *Use this page for additional lecture notes.*

UNIT 3

Apostles as Bondservants

UNIT CONTENTS
The Apostles' Commission
Apostleship & Diplomacy

UNIT GOAL

The goal of this unit is to study of the apostle's duty to submit to Christ as His bondservant and diplomat, and the irony of pairing the two terms.

UNIT OBJECTIVES

This unit has 5 objectives, which are:

- To show why the '**B**' in the series title stands for bondservant.
- To explain the uniqueness of the apostles' Commission.
- To establish the features of apostleship that differentiate it from ambassadorship.
- To show in active terms where apostleship looks a lot like ambassadorship in action.
- To address the '**D**' in the series title stands for diplomacy in apostleship.

> **UNIT TIDBIT:**
>
> "To show that apostleship is drastically different from secular ambassadorship, the apostle is called into service unquestionably as Jesus' slave."

SIGNIFICANT UNIT IDEAS TO STRESS:

The key discussion points of this unit are:

1. The second letter B, stands for Bondservant.
2. The meaning and mindset of a bondservant.
3. Why servant hood in general is essential for faithful apostleship and how it as a general term compares with a bondservant.
4. How the Lord Jesus demonstrated the attitude and character of a bondservant.
5. What it means to mistreat a powerful ruler's bondservant.

6. The third letter 'C' in the series title stands for Commissioned.
7. What a commission adds to traditional views and perspectives of apostleship.
8. Why apostles must be commissioned.
9. The fourth letter 'D' in the series title stands for Diplomacy.
10. What makes diplomacy a synonym for ambassadorship.

SCRIPTURE FOCUS

Throughout your study of this unit, you will focus on the following scriptures:

1. Joshua 9:4
2. 2 Chronicles 32:31, 35:21
3. Ephesians 6:20
4. Acts 26:12
5. Luke 14:31-33
6. Luke 19:14

UNIT KEYWORDS

The words you want to learn the most about in this unit are:

- Ambassage
- Bondservant
- Presbeia (G4242)
- Diplomacy
- Officiaries
- Commission
- Plenipotentiary
- Status vs. Rank
- Dignities
- Epitrope
- Statesmanship
- Assignment vs. Duty
- Duty vs. Responsibility
- government officials
- Government vs. Governance

WHAT YOU SHOULD KNOW OR BE ABLE TO DO FROM THIS UNIT

1. The ways that the word *apostleship* pertains to an apostle's *officiaries* and *dignities*.
2. The life of a bondservant of Jesus Christ, and the service of the one that is not.

3. How diplomacy works in general, and in apostleship in particular.
4. What makes a Christian minister a public servant and how God's ministries equate to kingdom service.
5. What the words <u>officiaries</u> and <u>dignities</u> mean in apostleship contexts.
6. The applied meanings of the Keywords.
7. How the Focus Scriptures were used.
8. What it takes to manifest the unit's goal.
9. What is involved in actualizing the unit's objectives.
10. How to embody the unit's subject matter usefully enough to share it with others.
11. Why apostles must liken themselves as Christ's slaves and how their doing so looks in action.
12. The importance of a commission to apostleship.

UNIT 3: SIGNIFICANT UNIT IDEAS TO STRESS

1. The second letter **'B'** that stands for Bondservant.

2. Who bondservants belong to.

3. The distinction of higher trained bondservants.

4. What makes apostles unquestionably see themselves as Jesus' slave.

5. How Jesus Christ modeled the bondservant side of His apostleship.

6. Why high level officials' bondservants were elevated by the status of their masters.

7. The third letter in our ABC's that stands for Commissioned.

8. The ways in which a commission dispatches an agent to represent an authority's as its official sent one.

9. How apostles fit the classification of a sent one.

10. The meaning and significance of the Greek New Testament word for commission, epitrope found in Acts 26:12.

11. How *epitrope* equates to a delegation of authority

12. The fourth letter D that stands for Diplomacy.

13. What makes diplomacy a synonym for ambassadorship, the ways both words amplify your understanding of apostleship.

14. Name the ways both words used above amplify your understanding of apostleship.

15. What it looks like to witness Diplomacy in action.

16. What makes diplomacy a governmental public service.

17. How diplomatic officials engage in negotiations and foster international relationships.

18. The reasons successful diplomacy depends upon skill in public affairs.

19. What managing people, resources, and institutions has to do with apostleship.

20. How statesmanship as an apostle's attribute facilitates kingdom diplomacy.

_____

_____

_____

_____

21. What makes diplomacy vital to God's reconciliation objectives.

_____

_____

_____

_____

KEYWORD STUDY: BONDSERVANT

> **Student**: *Use this study aid to help you gain a broader understanding of the keywords found in this unit. Apply each keyword in different ways to show how you recognize their relevance.*

Definition Study Chart		
Keyword or Term	**Definition: Source A**	**Definition: Source B**

List the scripture references related to your keyword(s):

Related Words Chart

Keyword or Term	Synonym(s)

Word Origins Chart

Origin of Term	Original Use	Modern Use	Scriptural Use

How is this word(s) used in this unit's study?

Term Purpose	Term Relevance	Skill Knowledge & Value

What is the scripture application?

What is their application to this unit study?

Summary Statement: *(Give a one-statement summary of what you have learned about your keywords and phrases)*

Three Main Revelations You Received:

What would you say is the value of this study to your, the Lord and His church?

KEYWORD STUDY: STATESMANSHIP

Student: *Use this study aid to help you gain a broader understanding of the keywords found in this unit. Apply each keyword in different ways to show how you recognize their relevance.*

Definition Study Chart		
Keyword or Term	**Definition: Source A**	**Definition: Source B**

List the scripture references related to your keyword(s):

Related Words Chart

Keyword or Term	Synonym(s)

Word Origins Chart

Origin of Term	Original Use	Modern Use	Scriptural Use

How is this word(s) used in this unit's study?

Term Purpose	Term Relevance	Skill Knowledge & Value

What is the scripture application?

What is their application to this unit study?

KEYWORD STUDY: COMMISSION

Student: *Use this study aid to help you gain a broader understanding of the keywords found in this unit. Apply each keyword in different ways to show how you recognize their relevance.*

Definition Study Chart		
Keyword or Term	**Definition: Source A**	**Definition: Source B**

List the scripture references related to your keyword(s):

Related Words Chart

Keyword or Term	Synonym(s)

Word Origins Chart

Origin of Term	Original Use	Modern Use	Scriptural Use

How is this word(s) used in this unit's study?

Term Purpose	Term Relevance	Skill Knowledge & Value

What is the scripture application?

What is their application to this unit study?

ACTION ITEM

What does an apostle as God's bondservant mean to you now, after having read this unit? How does this information change/alter your perspective? Why or why not?

SPECIAL UNIT END EXERCISE 1

Relating Scripture to Actions

God's Word on It

As God's Word on this unit, what about apostleship am I referring to below? Passages are taken from the KJV and the NKJV Bibles. Some passages repeat answers.

Straight from God's Word		
Your Answer Options		
Ambassador		
Ambassage		
Commission		
Ambassador		
Ambassador		
Messenger		
Delegation		
Scripture	**Answer**	**Explanation**
1. Joshua 9:4		
2. 2 Chronicles 32:31		
3. 2 Chronicles 35:21		
4. Ephesians 6:20		
5. Acts 26:12		
6. Luke 14:32		
7. Luke 19:14		

BONUS

This is a 2 part Assignment that may be given together or separately.

As a personal test of your new knowledge of apostleship, do the following assignment. If you are a class, you should receive extra credit for it, if your responses are good.

Part One: Depict illustratively how you see diplomacy, commission, and statesmanship all working together in modern apostleship.

Part Two: Specify using performance terms, how does the apostle's call to be a bondservant of Jesus Christ modify or regulate the 3 in active service?

SPECIAL UNIT END EXERCISE 2

Making Important Connections

Am I or Am I Not?

This is a common sense exercise to help you make important connections when applying this unit's subject matter. To complete it you will need your textbook, lecture notes, and the unit's key or significant points: Some of the terms from your keywords and others from the discussion points. The object is to select the best answer pair for the following rationales presented in the unit in respect to apostleship based on how apostles think and how you now perceive them. Choose your word pairs from the list below. They are not in any particular order and you can use a word more than once. Fill in the blanks with the words that make the most common sense to you after having completed the unit. You will have some words left over.

Exercise Word Choice List:

Independent	Bondservant
Diplomat	Statesman
Commissioned	Assigned
Private Citizen	Company Worker
Presbeia	Public Official
Sent One	Visitor
Ambassador	Government Official
Business	Status
Commission	Slave

1. If I am not _____, then I must be a _____.

2. If I am a _____, then I must also be a _____.

3. If I am not _____, then I must be _____.

4. If I am not _____ then I must be a _____.

5. To be a _____ is to not be a _____.

6. To be a _____ is to be an _____.

7. To be a _____ is to not be a _____.

UNIT 3: REVIEW QUESTIONS

To wrap up the study of this unit, answer the following questions.

1. The letter 'B' in the series title stands for_____.

2. Why does the word "bondservant" fit this study?

   _____

3. What scriptures did the unit use to illustrate the importance of apostles' seeing themselves as bondservants to Jesus Christ?

   _____

4. The group named in number 1 above belongs to who or what?

   _____

5. The highest trained members of the group you named in #1 usually do what?

   _____

6. In Romans 1:1, Paul places his status as bondservant above his _____

7. The third letter in our ABC's stands for _____?

8. The 5 things the unit taught that the third letter involves are:

   a.
   _____
   b.
   _____
   c.
   _____
   d.
   _____
   e.
   _____

9. How does your answer to #6 fit the apostle?

   _____

10. Explain three of the eight actions or features of the Greek word for #6.

    a.
    _____
    b.
    _____
    c.
    _____

d. _____

e. _____

11. What is the significance of the Greek word for commission to the unit's goal, and how do you see it reflected in the Unit's stated objectives?

_____

_____

_____

_____

_____

12. List 5 things that the two words the unit used to explain apostleship have in common.

a. _____

b. _____

c. _____

d. _____

e. _____

13. What makes the two words _____ and _____ useful to your to describe apostleship's primary function enlarge your appreciation of the office and its officer?

_____

_____

_____

14. The next letter in our series' alphabet is, "D". It stands for

_____.

15. How does the word you filled in above make apostleship a high profile public service to the Lord?

_____

_____

_____

_____

16. In what ways does an apostle's statesmanship demonstrate tactful handling of people?

_____

_____

_____

_____

17. How would you recognize apostolic statesmanship in action, and how essential is it for apostles of the Lord Jesus Christ sent out in His name?

_____

_____

_____

_____

BONUS

As a personal test of your new knowledge of apostleship, do the following assignment. If you are a class, you should receive extra credit for it, if your responses are good.

Depict how you see diplomacy, commission, and statesmanship all working together in modern apostleship and regulated by the apostle's call to be a bondservant of Jesus Christ.

UNIT 3: STUDENT LECTURE NOTES

Students: *Use this page for additional lecture notes.*

UNIT 4

Apostle vs. Apostleship

UNIT CONTENTS
Apostleship's History
Amazingly, Jesus Got Through

UNIT GOAL

The goal of this unit is to establish for you the distinct characteristics that make up the differences between the words apostle and apostleship, and show you how Jesus' message amazingly got through the muddle of false apostles' speaking for their deity's during His earthly ministry.

UNIT OBJECTIVES

This unit has 5 objectives, which are:

1. To solidify the difference and advantages of the all encompassing term apostleship over the word apostolic in action.
2. To assure that learners understand the importance and character of an office over the exercise of a gifting.
3. To show how and why offices regulate giftings and not the other way around.
4. To clarify the functional duties and objectives of an office.
5. To explain how to verify a true apostle, and why all apostles and ministers should be proved.

> **UNIT TIDBIT:**
>
> "Jesus' message produced *life*, **the major objective of true apostleship.**"

SIGNIFICANT IDEAS TO STRESS

The key discussion points of this unit are:

1. *Apostleship* and apostle are not the same and should not be treated as synonyms.
2. The reasons apostleship strictly pertains to the office.
3. Why offices need people in authority to staff them.
4. People appointed to offices are installed to represent their appointing authority's entity and not themselves.
5. Apostleship pertains to an area of authorized service to which a person is appointed by someone in authority.
6. Apostleship is validated by the credentials and stature of the person sent, the stature of the sender, and the weight of the commission message to be delivered, as well as the audience to whom it is addressed.
7. Secular apostles too circulated (and continue to circulate) messages from their gods.
8. Apostles as representatives of sovereigns and/or their deities must have a message.
9. The reasons Jesus' and His apostles' message got through to the Jews and the Gentiles and changed the world.
10. Jesus' and His apostles' message produced life, the major objective of true apostleship.
11. All apostles' messages and ministries should be thoroughly investigated according to the Bible's criteria and not just for its moral or ethical.
12. What scripture characterizes as an apostle is often at odds with what the modern church calls one.
13. Apostles should manifest God's Holy Spirit in truth.
14. The greatest effects of an apostle's ministry on your should be to draw you nearer to the Almighty God.
15. The uniqueness of biblical apostleship, as we will discuss thoroughly throughout this series, lies in the person of Jesus Christ and the power of His word as the Almighty's sent Messiah.
16. Christ's preaching and teaching never failed to manifest the Godhead's will, character, actions, and kingdom.

SCRIPTURE FOCUS

Throughout your study of this unit, you will focus on the following scriptures:

1. Acts 26:18
2. Matthew chapter 10
3. Luke 19:12-27
4. Acts 1:20
5. Romans 11:13
6. Luke 10:16
7. John 4:34; 6:38; 7:16-18
8. John 8:26

UNIT KEYWORDS

The words you want to learn the most about in this unit are:

- Message
- Life
- Discharge
- Charge
- Gifts
- Talents
- Spiritual
- Natural
- Endowments
- Agent
- Characteristics
- Institution
- Credentials
- Stature
- Messengers
- Sovereigns
- Deities
- Spokespersons
- Secular
- Manifestations
- Appointed
- Criteria

WHAT YOU SHOULD KNOW OR BE ABLE TO DO FROM THIS UNIT

To actualize your knowledge form this unit, you should embody the following things:

1. How the apostolic centers on the person and his or her gifts, talents, spiritual and natural endowments.
2. What apostleship really rests upon.
3. The official functions and duties of the apostle's office.
4. Apostleship's range of spiritual and natural responsibilities.
5. What your text means by "the offices predate those that enter them and impose immense changes upon their occupants."
6. Why giftings bestow less official powers on those that exercise them than an office does.
7. What the –ship at the end of apostle means and achieves.

8. How the suffix –ic differs from –ship in respect to apostles.
9. What an authorized area of service means and accomplishes for the Lord.
10. Apostleship is validated by its sender's credentials.
11. What is involved in discharging an office.
12. How duty, responsibilities, discharge and charge all pertain to an office.

UNIT 4: SIGNIFICANT IDEAS TO STRESS

1. The word apostleship differs from apostle.

2. What apostleship actually identifies.

3. The uniqueness of biblical apostleship.

4. The power in the Person of Jesus Christ, the Almighty's sent Messiah that electrified His message as heaven's sent one.

5. What made Jesus' and His apostle's message produce life, the major objective of true apostleship, and how it happened.

6. The objective of true apostleship and how to discern it when it appears.

7. How the Lord Jesus' message manifested the Godhead manifestations and why it was important that He did so.

COMPARISON CHART AND ANALYSIS

Apostolic vs. Apostleship

Activity Learning Value:

The learning value of this exercise is the heightening of your discernment faculties to skillfully detect the nuance difference in similar and dissimilar ideas, objects, and doctrine related to apostleship.

Instructions

Use your notes and discussion from Unit 4 to complete the following comparison analysis. Incorporate additional research and resources as necessary.

Suffices: "--ic" vs. "--ship"
Research the meanings of suffices "ic" and "ship". Bullet your findings in the space below.

--ic	--ship
Source(s):	Source(s):

Define the word apostolic:

Define the word apostleship:

Explain the differences between the two words

Scriptural applications of these terms:

What are the similarities?

What are the differences?

Sum up apostleship in one word:

UNIT 4: PRACTICE EXERCISE

Using your notes from Unit 4, your keyword study and comparative analysis chart as a guide, how might you explain the difference between apostleship and apostolic to a children's Sunday school class? Consider the following questions in developing your answer.

1. What is the most important thing they should know about the two terms?

_____

_____

_____

2. What kind of examples, illustrations, objects or comparisons would you use to help people understand your knowledge of apostleship?

_____

_____

_____

PART TWO: How would you alter your explanation of apostleship to help a group of teenagers understand it?

_____

_____

_____

1. What would you change?

_____

_____

_____

2. Why would you change anything?

_____

_____

_____

_____

3. What would tell you that you were successful?

_____

_____

_____

PART THREE: What would you do differently from your first two responses to make a person completely unfamiliar with apostleship appreciate it?

_____

_____

_____

_____

1. What would motivate you to vary your approach?

_____

_____

_____

2. What would signal to you that you needed to change your approach?

_____

_____

_____

_____

3. How would you know if your new way of sharing apostleship with the unexposed was successful?

_____

_____

_____

_____

NOTE: If you are a class, share all of your responses and critique one another's answers.

SPECIAL UNIT END EXERCISE

Relating Scripture to Actions

God's Word on It

As **God's Word** on this unit, what about apostleship am I referring to below? Why were these scriptures chosen in this unit? Choose the best word for the scripture passage. Some passages repeat answers Passages are taken from the KJV and the NKJV Bibles.

Straight from God's Word		
Your Answer Options:		
Apostle's as Ministry Official		
Apostles Give Life		
Apostle's Message		
Apostle's Service Type		
Apostle's Submission		
Apostleship Consciousness		
Apostle as Sent One		
Apostle's Commission		
Scripture	**Answer**	**Reason for My Choice**
1. Acts 26:28		
2. Matthew chapter 10		
3. Luke 19:19-27		
4. Acts 1:20		
5. Romans 11:13		
6. Luke 10:16		
7. John 4:34		
8. John 8:26		
9. John 10:10		

UNIT 4 REVIEW QUESTIONS

1. Apostleship and _____ are not the same.

2. What does the word apostolic not define?

_____

_____

3. What is the uniqueness of biblical apostleship?

_____

_____

4. Why must apostles have a message and where do they get their messages from?

_____

_____

5. What is the best way to verify God's apostles?

_____

_____

6. What was Jesus' message, and what did it produce?

_____

_____

7. What is an office?

_____

_____

8. True apostleship is _____. It touches:

    a. People

    b. _____

    c. Culture

    d. _____

9. Why do giftings not bestow the same weight of responsibility and authority as an office?

_____

_____

10. How would the Scripture Focus, if combined in a single statement, explain the power of apostleship and its basic message.

_____

_____

11. What would a person do to act out the unit's objectives?

_____

_____

12. In your opinion, based on what you have learned so far, what keywords best conveyed the unit's goal?

_____

_____

BONUS:

This is a two part assignment that may be given together or separately.

As a personal test of your new knowledge of apostleship, do the following assignment. If you are a class, you should receive extra credit for it, if your responses are good.

Part One: How would you observe, and recognize, Christ's brand of apostleship in action?

_____

_____

_____

_____

_____

_____

Part Two: How will your newfound apostleship revelation and insight influence your perspectives and dealings with God's apostles and the subject of apostleship in the future?

_____

_____

_____

_____

_____

_____

UNIT 4: STUDENT LECTURE NOTES

Students: Use this page for lecture notes.

UNIT 5

Reconnecting Apostleship with Your Biblical Roots

UNIT CONTENTS
Your Already Active Hidden Faith in Apostleship
Programmed Responses to Apostleship

UNIT GOAL

The goal of this unit is to bond you with the core premise of Apostleship's ABC's by making you comfortably understand apostles and trusting enough of the Lord's apostleship to trust your Christianity to it.

UNIT OBJECTIVES

This unit has 10 objectives, which are:

1. To introduce and familiarize you with the ministry and mantle of apostleship.
2. To reconnect you with apostleship's biblical roots and foundations.
3. To impress upon you eternity's passion for apostleship.
4. To surface your already existing faith in apostleship.
5. To instill in you an intimate firsthand knowledge of apostleship the way the Lord views apostleship.
6. To give you workable skillabilities for processing apostleship information and converting your thoughts and attitudes toward it.
7. To track for you the roots of apostleship's persecution.
8. To expose the theological preprogramming that fosters apostleship's persecution.
9. To paint a picture for you of God's ordained apostleship, how it looks in action, and what it accomplishes in the lives of those it touches.
10. To demonstrate for you the Lord's pressing need to reinstate apostleship.

SIGNIFICANT UNIT IDEAS TO STRESS

The key discussion points of this unit are:

1. The primary purpose of this book.
2. Your familiarity with apostleship and your intimate knowledge of its biblical place in the church and the world today.
3. The reason your genuine salvation and true faith in the Bible already makes you a believer in apostleship.
4. How and why apostles are definitely for today.
5. How and why God needs Christ's church to receive and respect His apostles.
6. How the Lord plans to populate the church with this office.
7. What makes apostles, as a rule, the Lord's best guardians.
8. The specific ways apostles are constructed and equipped to defend Christ in the church and the world.
9. Apostleship fears and errors are rooted in the early church's leadership's attempt at sparing the flock.
10. This systemized study was designed to overturn the affects of apostolic terrorism for you.
11. The first step is to successfully reinstating Christ's apostles at the head of His church is to redirect His people's manipulated and exaggerated fear of apostles to God's faith in them.

SCRIPTURE FOCUS

Throughout your study of this unit, you will focus on the following scriptures:

- Acts 14:19
- Acts 25:26
- Hebrews 3:1
- Ephesians 4:11
- Luke 6:13; 11:49
- 1 Corinthians 4:9, 10
- 1 Corinthians 12:28
- 2 Corinthians 6:3-10
- 2 Corinthians 11:16-33
- 2 Peter 2:3
- Jude 17

UNIT KEYWORDS

The words you want to learn the most about in this unit are:

- Salvation

- Guardian
- "Doctrend"
- "Apostolic Terrorism"
- Traditional
- Theological
- Mental Blank
- Attitude
- Exploit
- Exaggerated
- Persecution
- Rational vs. Irrational
- Tool vs. Instrument

WHAT YOU SHOULD KNOW OR BE ABLE TO DO FROM THIS UNIT

To actualize your knowledge form this unit, you should embody the following things:

1. The differences and similarities of the words apostle and apostleship.
2. The Bible's stance and teachings on apostleship.
3. What makes apostleship the foundation of all Christian ministry.
4. How most Christians' faith already rests in apostleship.
5. The damage that outdated commentaries and pulpit neglect or distortion of apostles has done to the Lord and His church.
6. What is involved in searching out the matter of apostleship for yourself.
7. How to become a rational thinking Christian on the subject of apostleship.
8. How to respond to the apostles that cross your path.
9. Theologically programmed responses to apostleship.
10. Prevailing attitudes toward apostleship and how they came to be.
11. The skillabilities you need to grasp, embrace, and effectively respond to your new apostleship knowledge.

UNIT 5: SIGNIFICANT IDEAS TO STRESS

1. The primary purpose of this book, as you have seen, is your familiarity with the term apostleship and your intimate knowledge of its biblical place in the church and the world today.

2. If you have a genuine salvation and true faith in the Bible, you are already a believer in apostleship.

3. This study will simplify for you why God needs Christ's church to receive and respect this office and how it must be reestablished as the viable guardian it is designed to be in mainstream Christian ministry.

4. When it comes to apostleship, both the fears and their errors stem from the early church's leadership's attempt at sparing the flock.

5. To remedy the situation, this systemized study was designed to overturn the affects of apostolic terrorism for you.

6. The first step is to redirect believers' fear of apostles to God's faith in them.

7. The unit posed 9 questions to give you a pretty reliable gauge for you to measure your personal knowledge and reactions to apostleship beyond what others have said to you.

8. Diligently search out apostleship truths for yourself.

9. Becoming a rational thinking Christian that learns to articulate intelligently your own issues with apostleship.

10. Being able to say why apostleship is needed or not, right ,or wrong for Christ church.

11. Should you should be served by an apostle or one of the other five-fold ministry posts?

12. Clearly and calmly expressing in your own informed words, your sentiments on apostleship.

13. The Lord's relentless drive to reinstate the apostle's office at the head of His New Testament church.

14. Conducting a diligent search of apostleship to uncover its truths in order to understand and embrace it based on your findings.

15. Apostles and apostleship have been viciously pummeled by the Lord's church for ages.

16. Numerous tactics have been used to persecute apostles and apostleship such as insufficient or biased theological commentaries and popular modern day "doctrends."

17. Countless horror stories are used to reinforce (or exploit) the error and fuel the fears that often unconsciously batters apostleship.

18. Due to its inaccurate portrayal and unjust treatment, true apostleship has been cloaked it in a terrifying garb that pummels it mercilessly and recycles its religious persecution.

19. God is summoning skillful apostles to reinstate this office for Him.

20. Using fresh revelation insightful thinkers are once more popularizing the Lord's rationale on apostleship.

UNIT 5: PRACTICE EXERCISE

How would you answer this Unit's Apostleship Self-Checker? In groups of four or more, have each group member answer the self-checker questions for themselves. When finished, swap papers anonymously and try to match the comment with the right group member.

Once each comment has been successfully matched, use the space below to identify five things you have learned about apostleship so far.

My Apostleship Self-Checker

When I hear the word *apostleship*...

- Do I wonder if apostleship has ever been mentioned in my church at all?

- Do I think about Jesus Christ, or just if it's a fad doctrine?

- Do I draw a mental blank?

- Do I think contemporary apostleship is biblical?

- Could I say what contemporary apostles look like, or how they act?

- How would I recognize an apostle on the street, or single one out in the church?

MY PERSONAL SUMMARY REVIEW

What I have learned about apostleship so far:

_____

_____

_____

_____

_____

_____

What I decided is the best way for me to share what I now know and understand about apostleship with others to help them understand its importance?

_____

_____

_____

UNIT 5: REVIEW QUESTIONS

1. Identify **five** things you have learned about apostleship so far:

1. _____

2. _____

3. _____

4. _____

5. _____

2. What makes you already a believer in apostleship?

_____

3. What does this unit refer to as the "first step" to reinstating apostleship?

_____

_____

4. What is a "doctrend"?

_____

_____

5. How does this formed word make our point about apostleship and traditional church teachings?

_____

_____

_____

6. The Lord is determined to restore apostleship in His church for what reasons?

_____

_____

7. Why should you be able to say rationally and calmly why apostleship should or should not exist, is or is not of God?

8. What would you say is involved in redirecting the modern Christian's fear of apostles to God's faith in them?

9. How would you lead someone that is susceptible to fear manipulations, especially regarding apostleship to become a rational thinking Christian?

10. What would you say is the one thought that convinces others that apostleship is not wrong for Christ's church?

11. How would you do your part to stop true apostleship from being mercilessly pummeled by religious persecution?

12. What would you say goes into popularizing the Lord's rationale on apostleship?

UNIT 5: STUDENT LECTURE NOTES

Students: Use this page for lecture notes.

UNIT 6

Biblical Foundations — Apostleship & God's Will

UNIT CONTENTS
Apostleship Obstacles
Jesus' Apostleship Mentality
Apostleship to God & Christ
Apostles as Guardians
Spiritual Flexibility
The Trickery of Impostor Deities

UNIT GOAL

To reveal and discuss the abundant biblical support that shows the Apostle's ministry as God's will and expose the tactics used to unseat Christianity as the number one world religion.

UNIT OBJECTIVES

This unit has 8 objectives, which are:

1. To identify for you apostleship's main obstacles
2. To show you how to confront apostleship myths
3. To give you signs of Spiritual Flexibility at work
4. To explore Jesus Christ's Apostleship Mentality as the Great Apostle
5. To explore the 'doctrends' at work against Christ and Christianity
6. To show you apostleship's value to God and Christ
7. To expose the Trickery of Impostor Deities
8. To identify apostleship's guardian role in God's kingdom for you

SIGNIFICANT UNIT IDEAS TO STRESS

The key discussion points of this unit are:

1. What apostleship means to God and Christ.
2. Apostleship is God's will.
3. The overwhelming biblical support for continued apostleship.
4. The 3 old womb barriers that hinder God's apostleship reinstatement campaign.
5. Five concrete reasons why apostleship exists to guard God's people and possessions.
6. Bible believing Christians must believe in apostles.
7. What makes apostles able guardians of God's church, faith, and kingdom.
8. The trickery of Impostor Deities
9. The damage done by irreverent ministers

SCRIPTURE FOCUS

Throughout your study of this unit, you will focus on the following scriptures:

- ◆ Ephesians 4:11
- ◆ 1 Corinthians 12:28
- ◆ Luke 11:49
- ◆ Ephesians 2:20
- ◆ Ephesians 3:5
- ◆ Revelation 18:20
- ◆ 2 Peter 3:2
- ◆ Jude 17
- ◆ Philippians 2:5
- ◆ Hebrews 13:17

UNIT FOCUS WORDS

The words you want to learn the most about in this unit are:

- ◆ Reinstatement
- ◆ Obstacle
- ◆ Refute
- ◆ Mindset
- ◆ Complacency
- ◆ Unorthodox
- ◆ Doctrine
- ◆ Mentality
- ◆ Crusade
- ◆ Charade

- Guardianship
- Godhead
- Mythical vs. Mystical
- Seductive
- Modernist
- Mystical Religion
- Spiritual Flexibility
- Biblical Christianity
- Self Shepherding
- Godly Guilt

WHAT YOU SHOULD KNOW OR BE ABLE TO DO FROM THIS UNIT

To actualize your knowledge form this unit, you should embody the following things:

1. The total biblical support scripture gives for apostleship.
2. The specific ways apostleship is God's will.
3. Apostleship's obstacles and what can be done about them.
4. How to confront apostleship myths.
5. The 3 old womb obstructions of apostleship.
6. How to explain apostleship's orthodoxy.
7. The absurdity of Christianity's rival doctrines
8. The 22 ideas Jesus that preoccupied Great Apostle on earth.
9. The best words to use to explain apostleship's value to God and Christ.
10. The five apostleship objectives.
11. The specific ways apostles guard Almighty God's interests.
12. Samples of seductive 'doctrends'.
13. What makes a religion mystical.
14. The signs and effects of an irreverent minister.
15. The discernible acts of spiritual flexibility.
16. What self shepherding looks and sounds like in action.

UNIT 6: SIGNIFICANT IDEAS TO DISCUSS

1. You should conduct your own Bible study to familiarize yourself with scriptures on apostles.

2. To date, many forerunners have labored to relay the biblical foundations for modern day apostleship.

3. Apostleship exists to guard God's people and possessions.

4. As popular doctrends would have it, unfaithful preachers modify many biblical patterns and eternal principles or suppress them to beguile the unenlightened.

5. Today countless believers are taught that the Bible is outdated and its righteousness standards irrelevant, no longer applicable to modern cultures.

6. Imposter deities commissioned Christ's opposers to use a devious ploy to seduce Christians to abandon His true faith.

7. Why traditionalist call apostleship teachings myths.

8. The "if God is eternal and perfect" persuasion the blocks anything new the Lord wants to do.

9. How unfaithful preachers modify many biblical patterns and eternal principles to suppress them and beguile the unenlightened.

10. The countless believers that are taught that the Bible is outdated and its righteousness standards irrelevant, no longer applicable to modern cultures.

11. The expressions of Jesus' Apostleship Mentality.

12. What apostleship does for God and Christ.

13. What about apostles that makes them able guardians for the Godhead.

14. How Imposter deities seduce Christians to abandon Christ's true faith.

15. The teaching on Spiritual Flexibility.

16. What reveals a Christian as being self-shepherded.

17. Why godly guilt is important and how it is encouraged in scripture.

18. How free will worship, religious liberty and interfaith all work against Christ and His church.

19. The ways the world wants to relegate Jesus to its pantheon of ancient deities and marry His faith to other religions.

UNIT 6: AUDIO/VISUAL WORKSHEET

LISTEN TO: The audio CD entitled "Apostleship is Gods and Nations." It is part of a CD series on the ABCs of Apostleship by Dr. Paula Price. As you listen to the CD, complete the worksheet below. (You may also listen to an apostolic teaching of your choice.)

Worksheet Complete Tips:

- ✓ Write down key words or phrases that you do not understand for quick look up after the teaching.
- ✓ Take notes while you are listening. This will help you to comprehend all that you heard and prepare you to fill out the worksheet.
- ✓ Pause the CD and rewind it as needed.
- ✓ Listen to the teaching several times.

ANSWER OR RESPOND TO THE FOLLOWING

Message Title: _____ **Date** _____

Question 1: What were three main points or ideas this teaching discussed? *(The main ideas were stated or presented in the teaching)*

1. _____

2. _____

3. _____

Question 2: Could you relate to the connections made on the tape between the message, its revelations, and the scripture passages used? Yes ☐ No ☐

Scripture	Saw Connection? Yes/No	What I learned and now Understand

Question 3: Did you identify what the teaching was meant to achieve?

_____

_____

Question 4: From what was taught, can you identify new information about the Lord and His church that you did not know before?

_____

_____

_____

_____

_____

Question 5: When you listened to the teaching, did its revelations or insights conflict with what you previously heard on the subject?

_____

_____

_____

_____

Question 6: Name three points made in the message that you found to be practical for everyday living. (*This question is looking for application—putting to use what you learned*)

1. _____
2. _____
3. _____

Use the space below to come up with five review questions for this message. These questions should be geared toward helping you pull the main ideas out of the teaching for yourself and for others.

1. _____
2. _____
3. _____
4. _____
5. _____

Question 7: Did you enjoy this teaching? Did you feel it was beneficial to your life? Why or Why not?

_____

_____

_____

_____

Question 8: In the space below, show how what you learned advanced your understanding of the teaching subject matter.

_____

_____

UNIT 6: TOPICAL SCRIPTURE STUDY

1 Corinthians 12:28

Activity Learning Value

To enable you to approach and explore scripture from an apostolic point of view. Requires you to inspect the assigned scriptures from God's word carefully to you match the appropriate wisdom to the situation that requires it.

Unit Recap:

Apostleship is God's will and scripture takes great pains to tell us so. Apostles are important to God because they guard His people, secure His best interests, and negotiate to His advantage in all affairs. (Refer again to **Philippians 2:5**).

Your Assigned Reading:
_____

Purpose of the Reading:
_____

How is the reading relevant to your study?
_____

What is the Reading's Knowledge/Skill Value?

Summarize Your Reading
_____
_____
_____
_____
_____
_____
_____

Write a General Statement Describing Your Reading

_____

_____

_____

_____

_____

_____

_____

_____

_____

Discuss Three Main Revelations You Received:

1. _____

2. _____

3. _____

_____

My Personal Experience with the ABC's Series

What I have learned about apostleship from this series:

_____

_____

_____

_____

_____

_____

What I have learned is the best way for me to share what I now know and understand about apostleship with others to help them understand its importance.

_____

_____

_____

SPECIAL UNIT END EXERCISE
Relating Scripture to Actions

God's Word on It

As **God's Word** on this unit, what about apostleship am I referring to below? Why were these scriptures chosen in this unit? Choose the best word for the scripture passage. Some passages repeat answers Passages are taken from the KJV and the NKJV Bibles.

Straight from God's Word		
Your Answer Options:		
Church Headship		
Apostles as Foundation Apostles' Word		
Soul Accountability		
Apostles' Commands Apostleship Revelation		
Apostles' Mind		
Ministry Offices		
Authorized Apostleship		
Apostles Avenged		
Scripture	**Answer**	**Reason for My Choice**
1. Ephesians 4:11		
2. 1 Corinthians 12:28		
3. Luke 11:49		
4. Ephesians 3:5		
5. Ephesians 2:20		
6. Revelation 18:20		
7. 2 Peter 3:2		
8. Jude 17		
9. Philippians 2:5		

SPECIAL PRACTICE EXERCISE

FILLING IN THE RIGHT WORD
Who Am I?

Activity Learning Value:

The learning value of this exercise is your recognition of and connection with the most effective apostolic words that distinguish apostleship from ambassadorship for others.

Using your book and lecture notes, enter the missing word or phrase in column 2 for each of the in column 1.

What I Do	Who Am I
1. I am paired with apostles in Ephesians 3:5	A.
2. I believe the Christian church should modernize.	B.
3. I take care of my own spiritual life.	C.
4. I get many to worship and serve me anonymously.	D.
5. I am what God wants next.	E.
6. I have a large ancient family tree.	F.
7. I beat out all of my contemporaries.	G.
8. I prove it is all about life.	H.
9. All I want is your worship.	I.

SERIES END BONUS

This is a three part assignment that may be given together or separately.

As a personal test of your new knowledge of apostleship, do the following assignment. If you are a class, you should receive extra credit for it, if your responses are good.

1. **Part One:** Say how your enlightened understanding of apostleship gained from this book of the ABC's transformed your beliefs and attitudes about apostleship.

2. **Part Two:** Describe in specific terms what you now comprehend apostleship to consist of and achieve for the Lord and His body.

3. **Part Three:** What is your present plan for encountering, working with and promoting apostleship as a result of these teachings?

UNIT 6: REVIEW QUESTIONS

1. List the scriptures that support apostleship

1. _____

2. _____

3. _____

4. _____

5. _____

6. _____

7. _____

8. _____

2. Explain in your own word how apostleship is God's will.

_____

_____

3. Give 3 reasons why God continues the apostle's office.

_____

_____

4. Describe the ways apostleship guards God's people and possessions.

_____

_____

5. Outline the sound, words, and effects of irreverent ministers.

6. Give an everyday example of the new move old womb conflict in action.

7. Say why do traditionalists call apostleship teachings myths?

8. Give your answer to the "if God is eternal and perfect" persuasion the blocks anything new the Lord wants to do from the text.

9. How do unfaithful preachers modify many biblical patterns and eternal principles or suppress them to beguile the unenlightened?

10. What makes countless believers say the Bible is outdated and its righteousness standards irrelevant?

11. What examples would you use show how people justify their feeling that the Bible no longer applies to modern cultures.

12. Summarize in your own words the 22 expressions of "Jesus' Apostleship Mentality" to share with others.

13. What are the 5 concrete objectives of apostleship?

1.

2.

3.

4.

5.

14. Give 3 things the unit taught that apostleship does for God and Christ.

15. What is it about apostles that make them able guardians for the Godhead?

16. Recall how Imposter deities seduce Christians to abandon Christ's true faith.

17. Summarize your comprehension of the teaching on Spiritual Flexibility.

18. Give some signs that reveal a self-shepherded Christian to you.

19. Why is godly guilt important and how it is encouraged in scripture?

20. How do free will worship, religious liberty and interfaith all work against Christ and His church?

21. Name the ways the world wants to relegate Jesus to its pantheon of ancient deities and marry His faith to other religions.

22. How do imposter deities deceive?

23. The primary focus of apostleship is: _____

24. How is God reinstating apostleship today?

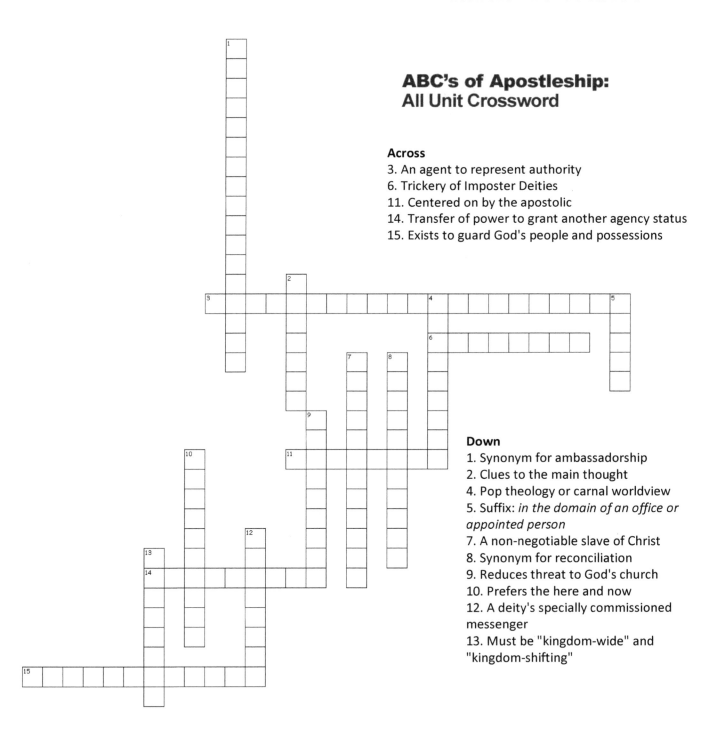

ABC's of Apostleship:
All Unit Crossword

Across
3. An agent to represent authority
6. Trickery of Imposter Deities
11. Centered on by the apostolic
14. Transfer of power to grant another agency status
15. Exists to guard God's people and possessions

Down
1. Synonym for ambassadorship
2. Clues to the main thought
4. Pop theology or carnal worldview
5. Suffix: *in the domain of an office or appointed person*
7. A non-negotiable slave of Christ
8. Synonym for reconciliation
9. Reduces threat to God's church
10. Prefers the here and now
12. A deity's specially commissioned messenger
13. Must be "kingdom-wide" and "kingdom-shifting"

My Study End Field Tester

HOW I PLAN TO FIELD TEST MY KNOWLEDGE

(Optional Knowledge Challenge)

Activity Learning Value: Field Testing My Knowledge

The learning value of this exercise is your ability to project how you will practically use what you have learned from this unit's[5] wisdom.

You will need your textbook, Bible, and lecture notes to complete this assignment.

Your Field Test Task
James 1:25

Create 5 or more questions from the unit (series or sessions) to ask the Subject Types you selected above. You can do this assignment by telephone, email, or in person. The goal of this exercise is your ability to prepare yourself to use what you just learned with real people who may or may not agree with you or be comfortable with your conversations on this subject. Here is how to do the exercise.

1. Prepare your questions on the lines below in column 1.
2. In column 2 write at least 2 anticipated responses to your question, one positive and one negative.
3. In column 3 prepare an answer to each one.
4. At the end of your form make some notes on your experience with each person to share with your classroom.
5. The class or study group should critique your results and discuss better questions, responses, and interview or communications techniques.

YOUR FIELD TEST SUBJECT TYPE	
1.	❏ The Enthusiast
2.	❏ The Skeptic
3.	❏ The Critic
4.	❏ Enlightened
5.	❏ The Believer
6.	❏ The Debater
7.	❏ The Analyst
8.	❏ The Timid
9.	❏ The Confused
10.	❏ The Universalist
11.	❏ The Traditionalist
12.	❏ The Minister

Can be given as a special or group project.

---

[5] Teachings or series.

The Exercise

My Question To This Subject Type: Your Question	The Answer I Anticipate from this Subject Type	My Answer Response to this Subject Type	Final Field Test Conclusions
1.			❑ Used training ❑ Ignored training ❑ Successful ❑ Unsuccessful ❑ Keep approach ❑ Change approach
2.			❑ Used training ❑ Ignored training ❑ Successful ❑ Unsuccessful ❑ Keep approach ❑ Change approach
3.			❑ Used training ❑ Ignored training ❑ Successful ❑ Unsuccessful ❑ Keep approach ❑ Change approach
4.			❑ Used training ❑ Ignored training ❑ Successful ❑ Unsuccessful ❑ Keep approach ❑ Change approach
5.			❑ Used training ❑ Ignored training ❑ Successful ❑ Unsuccessful ❑ Keep approach ❑ Change approach

How'd I Do With This Group?

END OF BOOK ONE

This is the end of Book 1 of your ABC's of Apostleship studies. I hope you enjoyed it and want to continue learning about apostles and their ministries. To advance to Book 2, you can go online at www.drpaulaprice.com to order it or call 918-446-5542. To proceed with your studies, you will need both the textbook and workbook.

ABOUT THE AUTHOR

Paula A. Price is a strong and widely acknowledged international voice on the subject of apostolic and prophetic ministry. She is recognized as a modern-day apostle with a potent prophetic anointing. Active in full-time ministry since 1985, she has founded and established three churches, an apostolic and prophetic Bible institute, a publication company, consulting firm, and global collaborative network linking apostles and prophets together for the purpose of kingdom vision and ventures. Through this international ministry, she has transformed the lives of many through her wisdom and revelation of God's kingdom.

As a former sales and marketing executive, Dr. Price effectively blends ministerial and entrepreneurial applications in her ministry to enrich and empower a diverse audience with the skills and abilities to take kingdoms for the Lord Jesus Christ. A lecturer, teacher, curriculum developer and business trainer, Dr. Price globally consults Christian businesses, churches, schools and assemblies. Over a 20-year period, Dr. Price has developed a superior curriculum to train Christian ministers and professionals, particularly the apostle and the prophet. Her programs often are used in both secular and non-secular environments worldwide. Although she has written over 25 books, manuals, and other course material on the apostolic and prophetic, she is most recognized for her unique 1,600-term *Prophet's Dictionary*, and her concise prophetic training manual entitled *The Prophet's Handbook*. Other releases include *Divine Order for Spiritual Dominance*, a five-fold ministry tool, and *Eternity's Generals*, an explanation of today's apostle.

Beyond the pulpit, Dr. Price is the provocative talk show host of her own program, *Let's Just Talk: Where God Makes Sense*. She brings the pulpit to the pew, weekly applying God's wisdom and divine pragmatism to today's world solutions. Her ministry goal is to make Christ's teachings and churches relevant for today. "Eternity in the Now" is the credo through which she accomplishes it.

In addition to her vast experience, Dr. Price has a D.Min. and a PhD in Religious Education from Word of Truth Seminary in Alabama. She is also a wife, mother of three daughters, and the grandmother of two. She presently pastors New Creation Worship Assembly in Tulsa, OK.

Introducing the Standardized Ministry Assessment Series
How do I test my Spiritual IQ?

Use our standardized ministry assessments to help determine where you fit—whether in ministry or business; find out how equipped you are for your calling, and evaluate your readiness. Our assessments are essential tools for Christian ministry that aid in assessing the potential and proficiency of those claiming or exhibiting ministerial aptitude or giftings in action.

Purpose for Destiny (PFD)

Have you ever asked yourself, "What was God thinking when He made me?" Are you a leader with members who seem like square pegs in round holes? If so, the Purpose for Destiny Questionnaire is ideal for you or your team.

Ministry Assessment Questionnaire (MAQ)

The MAQ is for any minister, leader, or gifted individual called to serve. It is an assessment created to identify the various features of five-fold ministry at work in an individual, as exhibited and/or practiced by the ministries featured in Ephesians 4:11 and I Corinthians 12:28-29.

Prophetic Aptitude Questionnaire (PAQ)

For prophets, intercessors, psalmists, seers, prayer warriors, and the like, the PAQ is an evaluative assessment tool to help Christian leaders evaluate those entrusted to their prophetic oversight or tutelage and to determine where their prophetic ministers may best serve. The PAQ is ideal for individuals interested in understanding their prophetic identity.

Apostolic Diagnostic Questionnaire (ADQ)

The ADQ is for apostles—seasoned and new; prophets—new and veteran; and pastors and church leaders inclined to apostolic ministry. It pinpoints whether you are called to serve officially in apostolic ministry or operate in the gifting. The AAQ reveals your strengths, weaknesses, and areas that need training and development.

What is the value of these assessments?

- Connect ministers with identity and calling

- Join leaders with a profitable tool for ministry selection

- Unite students with guidance and direction

- Link readiness programs with accurate evaluation of their trainees

For more information, visit www.drpaulaprice.com or call (918) 446-5542
to speak with an assessment representative.

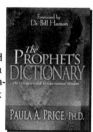

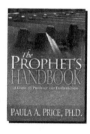

Printed in the USA
CPSIA information can be obtained
at www.ICGtesting.com
LVHW081041220124
769607LV00040B/909